To: _____

From: _____

New Seasons is a registered trademark of Publications International, Ltd.

© 2012 Publications Internaional, Ltd.
All rights reserved.
This publication may not be reproduced in whole or in part by any means
whatsoever without written permission from:

Louis Weber, CEO
Publications International, Ltd.
7373 North Cicero Avenue
Lincolnwood, Illinois 60712

www.pilbooks.com

Permission is never granted for commercial purposes.

Manufactured in China.

8 7 6 5 4 3 2 1

ISBN-13: 978-1-4508-3610-4
ISBN-10: 1-4508-3610-0

MOTHERS & SONS
Why Sons Always Need Their Mothers

Written by Dana Bottenfield

new seasons®

A SON NEEDS A MOTHER...

...to teach him when to lead and when to follow.

A SON NEEDS A MOTHER...

...to be there for his family.

A SON NEEDS A MOTHER...

...to keep traditions alive.

…to help him find his courage.

A SON NEEDS A MOTHER...

...to encourage brotherly love.

A SON NEEDS A MOTHER...

...to play with when it snows.

A SON NEEDS A MOTHER...

...to keep him close.

A SON NEEDS A MOTHER...

...to recognize accomplishments big and small.

A SON NEEDS A MOTHER...

...to give him a push to get himself started.

A SON NEEDS A MOTHER...

...to give him the tools to be independent.

A SON NEEDS A MOTHER...

...to show him how to dance.

A son needs a mother...

...to help him find balance in his life.

A SON NEEDS A MOTHER...

...to show him both patience and persistence.

A SON NEEDS A MOTHER...

...to make things all better.

A SON NEEDS A MOTHER...

...to retell his most triumphant moments.

A SON NEEDS A MOTHER...

...to show him how to treat a friend.

A SON NEEDS A MOTHER...

...to find what's special in each of us.

A SON NEEDS A MOTHER...

...to show him how to take
care of the world around him.

A SON NEEDS A MOTHER...

...to show him that you should
always have a sense of humor.

A SON NEEDS A MOTHER...

...to teach him how to drive.

A son needs a mother...

...to set boundaries in his life.

A SON NEEDS A MOTHER...

...to provide an honest and fair opinion.

A SON NEEDS A MOTHER...

...to help him stay true to himself.

A SON NEEDS A MOTHER...

...to show him how to be a straight-shooter.

A SON NEEDS A MOTHER...

...to help him celebrate his birthday.

A SON NEEDS A MOTHER...

...to hold him up until he can support himself.

A son needs a mother...

...to give him safety and warmth.

...to let him rock out.

A SON NEEDS A MOTHER...

...to show him how to spread his wings.

A SON NEEDS A MOTHER...

...to encourage his creativity.

A SON NEEDS A MOTHER...

...to teach him about the world around him.

A SON NEEDS A MOTHER...

...to welcome his new family.

A SON NEEDS A MOTHER...

...to teach him life's most important skills.

A SON NEEDS A MOTHER...

...to teach him street smarts.

A SON NEEDS A MOTHER...

...to walk him through his first steps.

A son needs a mother...

...to help him make wishes for the future.